SUPER CUTE!

Baby Sea Otters

by Christina Leaf

BELLWETHER MEDIA · MINNEAPOLIS, MN

Note to Librarians, Teachers, and Parents:

Blastoff! Readers are carefully developed by literacy experts and combine standards-based content with developmentally appropriate text.

Level 1 provides the most support through repetition of high-frequency words, light text, predictable sentence patterns, and strong visual support.

Level 2 offers early readers a bit more challenge through varied simple sentences, increased text load, and less repetition of high-frequency words.

Level 3 advances early-fluent readers toward fluency through increased text and concept load, less reliance on visuals, longer sentences, and more literary language.

Level 4 builds reading stamina by providing more text per page, increased use of punctuation, greater variation in sentence patterns, and increasingly challenging vocabulary.

Level 5 encourages children to move from "learning to read" to "reading to learn" by providing even more text, varied writing styles, and less familiar topics.

Whichever book is right for your reader, Blastoff! Readers are the perfect books to build confidence and encourage a love of reading that will last a lifetime!

This edition first published in 2014 by Bellwether Media, Inc.

No part of this publication may be reproduced in whole or in part without written permission of the publisher. For information regarding permission, write to Bellwether Media, Inc., Attention: Permissions Department, 5357 Penn Avenue South, Minneapolis, MN 55419.

Library of Congress Cataloging-in-Publication Data

Leaf, Christina, author.
  Baby Sea Otters / by Christina Leaf.
    pages cm. – (Blastoff! Readers. Super Cute!)
  Summary: "Developed by literacy experts for students in kindergarten through grade three, this book introduces baby sea otters to young readers through leveled text and related photos"– Provided by publisher.
  Audience: Ages 5-8.
  Audience: K to grade 3.
  Includes bibliographical references and index.
  ISBN 978-1-60014-976-4 (hardcover : alk. paper)
  1. Sea otter–Infancy–Juvenile literature. 2. Animals–Infancy–Juvenile literature. I. Title.
  QL737.C25L4 2014
  599.769'5'139–dc23
                            2013050356

Table of Contents

Pups!

Baby sea otters
are called pups.
They are born in
the ocean.

Life With Mom

A mom has only one pup. It needs all of her care!

The pup cannot swim yet. Mom hugs it close.

Thick fur helps the pup float. Mom **grooms** this fluffy coat often.

The pup goes everywhere with mom. It sleeps on her belly.

Time to Eat

Newborn pups drink mom's milk. Older pups share her food.

Young pups learn
how to crack
open **shellfish**.

Mom dives to find more food. The pup waits for her to return.

Mom wraps the pup in **kelp**. Then it will not float away. Hold on tight!

Glossary

grooms—cleans

kelp—large weeds that grow in ocean water

newborn—just born

shellfish—animals with hard outer shells that live in the ocean; sea otters eat shellfish such as mussels and clams.

To Learn More

AT THE LIBRARY

Gates, Margo. *Sea Otters*. Minneapolis, Minn.: Bellwether Media, 2014.

Levine, Ellen. *Seababy: A Little Otter Returns Home*. New York, N.Y.: Walker & Co., 2012.

Owen, Ruth. *Sea Otter Pups*. New York, N.Y.: Bearport, 2013.

ON THE WEB

Learning more about sea otters is as easy as 1, 2, 3.

1. Go to www.factsurfer.com.

2. Enter "sea otters" into the search box.

3. Click the "Surf" button and you will see a list of related web sites.

With factsurfer.com, finding more information is just a click away.

Index

The images in this book are reproduced through the courtesy of: Minden Pictures/ SuperStock, front cover, pp. 4-5, 6-7; Bill Rome/ Alaska Stock-Design Pics/ SuperStock, pp. 8-9; Milo Burcham/ Alaska Stock-Design Pics/ SuperStock, pp. 10-11; Steven Kazlowski/ Science Faction/ SuperStock, pp. 12-13; Tom & Pat Leeson/ Agefotostock, pp. 14-15, 16-17; Kevin Schafer/ Nature Picture Library, pp. 18-19; Doc White/ Nature Picture Library, pp. 20-21.